C000058295

Successful Social Life

Other titles in this series
(all by Susan Quilliam):

Body Language Secrets:
Successful Social Life

Susan Quilliam

Thorsons
An Imprint of HarperCollins*Publishers*

Thorsons
An Imprint of HarperCollins*Publishers*
77–85 Fulham Palace Road,
Hammersmith, London W6 8JB
1160 Battery Street,
San Francisco, California 94111-1213

Published by Thorsons 1996
10 9 8 7 6 5 4 3 2 1

© Transformation Management 1996

Susan Quilliam asserts the moral right to
be identified as the author of this work

A catalogue record for this book
is available from the British Library

ISBN 0 7225 3126 5

Printed in Great Britain by
Woolnough Bookbinding Limited, Irthlingborough

All rights reserved. No part of this publication may be
reproduced, stored in a retrieval system, or transmitted,
in any form or by any means, electronic, mechanical,
photocopying, recording or otherwise, without the prior
permission of the publishers.

To Desmond Morris – who else?

Contents

Acknowledgements

I would first like to acknowledge the many sources and individuals who helped me gain my research material, particularly the staff of the Open University Library, the staff of the University of London Library, and Felicity Sinclair. A special acknowledgement to Samantha Smeraglia for her ability to collate my research so wonderfully!

My thanks also to: Barbara Levy, my agent, for her continued support; Sharon Scotland, the illustrator; to Jane Graham-Maw, Michele Turney, Jenni Maas and Barbara Vesey from

Thorsons for making the writing and production of this book such an enjoyable experience; to my personal assistant June Bulley for her constant administrative excellence.

A final thank you to my husband Ian who, as always, makes all things possible.

Throughout this book, the people referred to could be either 'he' or 'she'. Consistently referring to one gender would not only raise political issues, but would be unfair to the 'other kind'! In general, therefore, unless to do otherwise would make the text inaccurate, I have alternated pronouns in successive questions in this book, to give a balanced feel.

Preface

Before you read this book, remember that body language:

- is every kind of human behaviour *except* the words spoken – from gestures to breathing, from the way muscles move to a person's use of time
- is not able to tell you everything – you may need the words too
- does not let you read everyone like a book – because everyone has his or her own personalized body language
- will not give you power over people – they will not respond unless they want to

- will not work if you try to change others
  – you can only ever shift what *you* do and
  alter the situation that way
- is about gathering information – you will
  be more successful if you do
- is something you already know – your
  natural body language works best
- is best tried out slowly and carefully
  – new body language patterns can look
  false
- works by trial and error: do more of what
  succeeds, and stop doing anything that
  doesn't!

How Can Body Language Help Me Build My Social Life?

Over 90 per cent of what people communicate to each other is nonverbal. So it goes without saying (as it were) that if you do not pay attention to body language, your relationships will always be less rewarding than they could be.

Body language first of all helps you understand people. Above and beyond the words, you can tell what others are really saying, interpret what they are trying to say, uncover what they are trying not to say. You can look at the way people stand, the gestures they make, the expressions on their faces, the way they speak – and use all that to build up a rounded picture of someone as a person, or a quick snapshot of him or her in a particular situation.

You can also adapt your own body language to be more successful with people. Rather than simply listening or talking, unaware of the impact you are making, you can start to choose to give people the body language messages you want to – that you are pleased to see them, that you are feeling bored, or that you want to see them again. Particularly, you can be aware of when you are making a bad impression, and put that right as soon as possible.

Recent research has developed a great deal of knowledge about body language in groups. So you can use body language particularly to analyse what is really happening under the surface during meals, at parties, when playing sport. And you can become much better able to make group events go well, because all the nonverbal elements such as the place, the time, the scene-setting will be right.

Your social life is important – so it's important to get it right. Whether in one-to-one friendships or in groups of friends, whether with perfect strangers or with people you have known for years, body language gives you extra tools with which to do just that.

What Really Happens When I Meet Someone New?

When you meet someone for the first time – at a party, in the pub, on the street – you become a video camera. You take a snapshot, with your eyes and ears. You scan, with eye movements so fast that they are practically unnoticeable, the most obvious details of the newcomer – height, weight, skin colour, clothes. Your ears respond to the first sounds of his (or her) voice, taking in accent, tone and volume levels. And within the first crucial ten seconds of even glimpsing someone, you use this snapshot to make an instant assessment. What a person looks like tells you how to think, feel and behave towards him.

If your new acquaintance is tall, for example, research shows that you will tend to think that he is both intelligent and successful. If this person is smaller than you are, on the other hand, you will be tempted to view him as ineffectual (if a man) or slightly helpless and in need of protection (if a woman). If the stranger is above normal weight, you may see him as easy-going, but lazy. If your new acquaintance is attractive – or at least, matches the current fashionable image of attractiveness in terms of physique and dress – then you are likely to expect him to be confident and at ease.

If she is female, you will expect her to be socially welcoming, and so you may smile and move forward; if he is male, you will expect him to be more confronting and assertive, so may stay back. And if the newcomer's gender is unclear – a man wearing kohl eyeliner or a woman with a masculine figure – then studies show that you will get confused, irritated and anxious.

Perhaps the most basic assessment you make about a new acquaintance concerns 'status'. In other words, is he more 'important' than you are? Some nonverbal status symbols in Britain at present are: being a man, being older, being expensively dressed, having a standard (i.e., southern) English accent. So, for example, if a newcomer is obviously much older than you, you will probably act as if he is also 'wiser', perhaps letting him speak first, being more likely to agree with him, nodding as he makes his points.

There is only one problem: These reactions to another person's nonverbal appearance are not only instinctive and instant. They are also very often quite inaccurate. Not all people above average weight are lazy. Not all beautiful people are necessarily confident.

And here is the twist, of course: While you are judging other people on their appearance, they, of course, are judging you on yours. The assumptions you make about others are just as likely to be the assumptions they make about you ...

What Do I Do When I Begin an Interaction – with Different People?

First contact is often the most important part of any interaction. The moment you greet someone, you reveal your attitude, your mood – even your personality. You do this by five key things in your body language: your posture, your facial expression, your movements, your tone of voice, your touch. All these combine to give the person you greet a distinct impression of you. For example ...

Are you giving the impression of formal respect – perhaps to a boss, or the bank manager? Formal body language is all about being direct, controlled but a little distant. So you may take up a straight posture, facing the other person head on but standing back and keeping your distance. A formal smile is pleasant but brief, often with lips closed rather than the more informal smile that shows your teeth. A formal tone of voice is low, slow and steady, giving an impression of confidence and competence because it does not let any emotional insecurity show. And formal touch – though vital to create trust – is limited, often just an arm's-length handshake.

But say you are greeting a friend in the pub. Here your approach changes completely. You already know the other person, so your body language can be much more casual. You just glance briefly, give a 'greeting' nod and smile. You may not face the other person directly or touch in greeting, because the relationship is

already established (unless of course, you are French, a nationality that shakes hands compulsively every time they pass each other in the street!). On the other hand, it is also much more acceptable to let your body language reveal your emotions, even your negative feelings. So you may well frown with anxiety, slam down your glass in frustration or let your tone of voice show just what a rotten day you have had.

Different again is greeting someone you want to build a close relationship with – perhaps a friend's new partner or a member of a new partner's family. Here you do not want to be formal, but cannot afford to be casual; you want to forge strong and positive links. You lean towards the other person to show you are interested. You smile with the genuine smile that reveals your teeth and wrinkles your eyes.

You use open, 'inclusive' gestures that tell the other person that you want her (or him) to be part of your life. And you use touch to create and reinforce the link between you, with a double hand clasp, a lingering pat on the shoulder, a kiss on the cheek. Getting as close as you can, you forge a bond at the start that will make you feel good about each other for a long time to come.

What Is the Secret of Being a Good Listener?

A good listener is a mirror – not a blanket or a brick wall. Some people, the 'blankets', constantly interrupt the flow of the other person's conversation with their own nonverbal signals – shifting, blinking, looking away. The brick walls, on the other hand, give nothing back; they stand quiet and motionless, making no response, until the talker simply dries up and falls silent.

But if you are listening well, your body language is a mirror of what the other person is saying. So begin by using the 'mirrors' of

the soul, the eyes, to look at the other person, showing your interest in him (or her) and his words. Do not worry if he looks away – he may have to in order to think – but keep your gaze on his face, and mark your visual interest further by making sure that the rest of your body is inclined in his direction too. Good listeners also tend to tilt their head slightly, because jaw angle actually affects the ability to hear better; so let your head naturally angle to one side.

Also, use the universal sign of acknowledgement, the nod of the head. An effective nod is usually hardly noticeable, but it is another kind of mirror, naturally happening at just the point where the speaker gets most animated – where he puts stress on a particular vital word or where he gestures strongly to make a point. If the speaker then

says something even more important, you may
find yourself giving a longer, slower nod of
the head, suggesting that you are taking him
just that bit more seriously.

You can add to this message by picking up on
what the other person is feeling and, in your
role as 'mirror', reflecting it back to him. This
does not mean howling with laughter if he
merely smiles; but smiling when he laughs,
taking on a sympathetic expression when he
talks about something sad, frowning with
empathetic irritation when he gets angry.
These emotional reflections give the message
'I can feel some of what you are feeling.
I understand.'

Good listening obviously involves asking
questions. But a question thrown in when the
speaker is not ready is worse than no question

at all. So before you query, watch for the natural break, signalled by the speaker's slowing down, letting his voice rise or fall in pitch, looking directly at you as if appealing for a response, giving an open-palmed movement that says 'It's your turn now.'

In return, your question can be accompanied by a head tilt, a slight smile, a raise of the eyebrows: the body language that gives the reassuring message: 'I don't disagree with you ... I just want to know.' Then, as you reach the end of your question, hand back to the speaker with a direct look and that turn-giving, open-handed gesture mentioned before.

How Can I Really Involve Listeners in What I Am Saying?

Talking is not only about the words. When you speak, you also communicate through your body. And if you want to involve others in what you are saying, you need to use body language that involves them too.

Begin by letting your posture and expression show that you are aware of the other person. Turn fully towards her (or him); this tells her you are interested in making contact and allows her to get the most amount of information as you speak. Use wide 'inclusive' movements that say 'I want to involve you in what's happening.' And although you will regularly need to look away while speaking in order to think about what to say next, always re-establish contact with your listener by looking back at her at regular intervals.

The next step is to let your fingers do the talking. Effective speakers use gestures to communicate fully with their audience, emphasizing, explaining, clarifying – Italians, that most involving of nations, can actually become speechless if asked to sit on their hands! So become aware of the natural gestures you use and then make them clearer, more definite, more relevant to what you are saying.

You might use a 'baton' gesture. This is a downwards or sideways movement of the hand, so-called because it beats out the important points of your conversation just as a conductor's baton beats out key musical rhythms. You may use a 'metaphor' gesture, to draw out in the air a picture of what you really mean – curving your hands perhaps to indicate that you feel something is unified or complete, pushing your palms downwards if you are talking about a drop in noise or emotion. Or you may use 'punctuation' gestures to show that you have come to the end of a point; waving a hand with palm down to finish a statement, turning your hand palm up to invite the other person to talk for a while.

Also, use your voice to draw the listener in. Have a clear, confident tone that is not anxiously nasal, or breathless. Adopt a speed that is fast enough to keep up interest, but slow enough to be understandable. Use the rhythm of your voice to stress the words that are important to you in what you say. And remember that if you occasionally lower your voice just a fraction, or even pause for a moment, a person will automatically listen more carefully to you for the next few sentences.

Some speakers can say the most wonderful things – but their listeners feel alienated because their body language is static or rejecting. Using all your body skills to enthuse and include people will mean that they take what you say more seriously, and respond to it much more positively.

Can I Tell from Other People's Body Language Whether I Will Get On with Them or Not?

The answer to this question is both yes and no. If you try to judge whether you will get on with someone from the shape of his (or her) hands or the position of his legs, you will almost always get it wrong. The uncontrollable, genetic elements of a person's body, such as the shape of his hands, have no direct link with what kind of person he is. And short-term body language, such as temporary leg position, always has to be interpreted in the particular context in which you see it.

But if a person regularly thinks and feels a particular way, and therefore consistently stands, moves or even grimaces in specific body patterns, then his body will naturally tend to fall back into those same patterns. So if you really want to understand someone else, look at his normal 'resting' posture, the one he falls back into naturally. Look at the spontaneous tilt of his head. Examine his facial lines, where decades of fleeting expressions have etched their most common expressions firmly into place. Notice his regular, repeated sequences of movement – the way he walks, sits or breathes. Get a rounded picture of someone's body patterns and you will get a rounded picture of who he is.

For example, is the person you are with easy-going? Is his natural posture relaxed? Is

he at home with people – does he naturally
turn his head towards you, seeking your
company? Is he optimistic – does he have
natural 'smile lines'? Is he energetic and alert
– are his movements habitually direct,
rhythmic and well-paced?

Once you have made your analysis, how can
you decide whether this person is someone you
could get on with? As a general rule, ask
yourself whether you feel at ease with what
you see and what you sense. If so, it is likely
that the other person's body language is within
a range that roughly matches your own.

That is not to say that you are both totally
easy-going, or completely optimistic. But if
you are moving at very different speeds or
sitting in very different postures, you may find
that you automatically feel ill at ease. Your

natural body language, which is the tip of the iceberg as far as your personality and attitudes are concerned, is quite dissimilar – and should sound a warning bell.

If, on the other hand, there is a basic similarity between you in body language, then this is proof positive that you are reaching a real rapport. And this in turn means that it is highly likely that you will get on well in the future.

Can I Tell from Other People's Body Language Just What They Are Feeling?

Primitive humans often faced a problem such as an attacking animal, or an opportunity such as a tree full of ripe fruit. Then they not only geared up for action with a rush of adrenalin and an increase in breathing rate, they also signalled their reactions on the outside, to alert other members of the tribe to what was happening.

Nowadays we call this kind of physiological reaction an 'emotion'. We feel anxiety when facing a roomful of strangers rather than an attacking beast, and we feel excited when looking forward to a good night out rather than a meal from a fruit tree. But the basic emotional responses we feel are the same as ever, and the body language signals we send out are also very similar.

Nowadays, though, human beings are often trained not to show emotions – anxiety, irritation, sadness, surprise, delight. So while someone might reveal her (or his) real feelings to her family, friends or to an intimate partner, when she is in a purely social situation she may well try to conceal her mood. This means that if you want to understand how someone is really feeling – confident, anxious, irritated, satisfied – you may have to look carefully.

The key is facial expression. Human eyes, eyebrows and mouth are the features that originally transmitted the crucial signals about a potential threat or benefit to the tribe. And human faces still give off signals of emotion so universal and cross-cultural that many are exactly the same in an uptown New Yorker as in a Kalahari Bushman.

So a slightly open mouth, open alert eyes and raised eyebrows will signal a sense of surprise or fear, as if the person is intent on spotting and monitoring a possible threat. A downturned mouth and sunken eyes will indicate sadness or disappointment; if tears are on the way, watch for the eyes reddening and a gleam of moisture along the lower lid. Anger or aggression uses a pushed forward mouth and staring eyes, as if to challenge an enemy; the eyebrows may be lowered and drawn together, which in monkeys indicates an urge to attack. And a happy or contented person will show, however slightly, a smile that turns the corners of his mouth up and creases the muscles round his eyes.

Very often you will actually see a mixture of these signals. This will happen particularly in situations where it is just not acceptable to express strong critical emotions such as anger or disappointment. So if you see conflicting signals – a smiling mouth but glowering eyes, for example – what you may be glimpsing is anger masked by acceptance. If you recognize this, and so understand what is really happening, you will handle the person – and the situation – much better.

What Can Others' Eye Movements Tell Me About Them?

You may have noticed that as a person thinks, his (or her) eyes move. A friend may look at you when you are talking. But when he is talking – and has to think about what he is saying – he will often look away, and in different directions – upwards, sideways, downwards. If he looks upwards or downwards, he may well tilt his head in that direction too; if he looks sideways, he may angle his head to one side as he does so.

Research by U.S. psychologists Richard Bandler and John Grinder now seems to

indicate that when someone's eyes move like that, it shows that he is thinking in particular ways. To understand this, first remember that the two senses that we, as humans, mainly use are those of sight and hearing. We not only see and hear things; we also think in pictures and in sounds. (If you question that, try remembering first what your front door looks like, and secondly what your front door key sounds like as you put it in the lock; you will be able to recall these things, however vaguely, as a picture and a sound.)

Bandler and Grinder suggest that if a person looks upwards, then he is thinking about a sight; he has a picture of something in his head, is visualizing it in his mind's eye. If he glances to the side, he is thinking about a sound; he is maybe remembering a remark someone passed, or some music he is fond of, and is visualizing it in what we might call 'the mind's ear'.

Further, if someone consistently looks in one direction – for example, upwards – that means that he thinks mainly in pictures and makes visual images of what he is thinking about. It also means that he is likely to remember what he sees very fully, that he will have a vivid, visual imagination and that he is likely to be good at things that require a strong visual sense.

If someone tends to look mainly sideways, that indicates that he thinks mainly about what he hears. He is likely to remember best what he has heard, will be able to imagine sounds and words very clearly and is likely to be good at things that need a strong sense of sound or rhythm.

48

The research on which these ideas are based is new but exciting. Trained workers in the field claim to be able to map people's thought processes in some detail and with some accuracy. Without that training, you cannot really tell what people are thinking about second to second – though of course you can always ask when you see them glancing away.

What you can do, though, is start to get an insight about the way people experience the world. Take that friend mentioned at the start of this section; is he sight-orientated, or sound-orientated, a looker or a listener? And what does that mean about the sort of person he is?

Lookers have a good visual sense and may need to see you in order really to relate. Listeners love music and all kinds of sound;

49

they often have a good sense of rhythm. If you are chatting to a friend about something that happened, a looker will need you to build a picture that he can see in his mind's eye. The listener, on the other hand, will not need any descriptions but will enjoy the telling of the tale itself, a blow-by-blow account of what happened, when and in what order.

If it comes to buying presents, remember whom you are buying for. Your looker friend will want his gift beautifully wrapped, and will welcome anything that looks good and has visual style. Your listener friend will go into ecstasies over a record, or spoken-word books featuring the voices of great actors, but will not actually worry about the visual presentation. He will not even care too much if you wrap your gift in a brown paper bag!

How Can I Spot that I Am Boring People – and What Should I Do If I Am?

Unless you are being incredibly dull, then it may be quite difficult to spot that you are being boring. For it is not really socially acceptable for other people to admit they feel uninterested, or to show clear signs of boredom. People try to neutralize their body language so that others will not be offended by their reaction.

Perhaps the initial thing to be aware of, then, is whether the person opposite you is looking blank. She (or he) may go very still, stop making gestures, stop moving as she listens to you – all to hide her irritation and frustration. The other reason that a bored companion might suddenly go still and blank-faced is that in conversation, tiny movement signals such as smiles and nods are a listener's way of encouraging the speaker to go on and say more. If the person you are with does not actually want you to say more, then she will naturally cut down on those signals.

On the other hand, a bored person can move even more than usual – for comfort. People under stress have been shown to reduce tension by minute body shifts, which are possibly a comforting reminder of when, as children, we were rhythmically rocked by our mother's motions. Feet movements can also be interpreted as 'escape' movements, where the body tries to flee but cannot. If you see 'feet flurries' along with a body leaning towards the door or an unconscious turn of the head towards the exit, then you may have good reason to suspect that your companion simply wants to be gone!

What can you do? First, check if the other person's boredom is because something else, somewhere else, looks more interesting to her. If it is not actually you that is off-putting, but the view in the mirror behind you that is attractive, then move so that you alone are in the other person's line of sight. Shift so that your body is blocking her off from all distractions. Then reach out and touch her, perhaps reclaiming her attention by saying her name – the single sound that adult humans respond to most readily.

Or, allow your companion to do some of the talking. Is she giving you 'turn-demanding' signals – looking intently at you, nodding rapidly to hurry you up, taking a breath as if to speak as soon as you slow down? If so, be democratic. Bring your sentence to a close, ask a question about your listener's thoughts, and let her have her turn. You may find that her boredom signals instantly disappear!

How Can I Tell If People Really Find My Jokes Funny?

Amusement affects the whole of a person's body. It stimulates every organ in a way that has been described as 'stationary jogging', exercising the face, neck, shoulders, stomach and diaphragm. It reduces blood-pressure, increases the amount of oxygen in the blood, lowers the heart rate, boosts the immune system, even stimulates the body's natural painkillers, beta-endorphins. Laughter is, in fact, the best medicine.

What occurs on the surface of the body during amusement is just as dramatic. The impact inside almost always makes a person move around, even if only slightly. If very amused, he (or she) will shake with laughter. His breathing will quicken and he will often gasp for breath. He may even reach out as if for support to the person next to him. He will change colour, turning red because the amusement has expanded the blood vessels close to the surface of his skin.

If someone responds to a joke you tell as strongly as described above, then you can be certain that you have hit home. But what if the response is a little more low key? People do fake amusement, so as not to upset the joke-teller. How can you spot when someone is faking for you?

The main sign of real amusement, the one that a person just cannot fake, is the genuinely amused smile. A real smile comes quickly. It is synchronized with the joke to within $\frac{1}{48}$th of a second, or sometimes even slightly before it, as the listener's mind makes the final leap ahead of the last syllable of the punch line. A real smile is symmetrical, equal on both sides of the face; it comes quickly and fades slowly. It curves upwards and brings into play the lines that run from the corner of the nose to the corner of the mouth (the naso-labial folds). It also involves the eyes, which crinkle slightly as the muscles around them respond to the smile.

No one can fake any of these movements, of mouth or of eyes; they are not under conscious control. So a faked smile comes slowly, dies away slowly, and is slightly imbalanced, as if one side of the face is aiming for a positive response while the other side is not too sure. A faked smile tends to be oblong rather than curved, because the smile muscles along the naso-labial folds are not really being used. And the eye muscles are not fully brought into play – which is why the cold, villainous smile of the movie 'baddie' never reaches his eyes.

Should you catch any of these signs of a false response, you may want to change your line in jokes – or tell them to a more appreciative listener!

What Are the Nonverbal Signs of a Really Good Friendship?

When you first make friends with someone, it is a bit like love without the sex. Adrenalin rushes through your body, your heart beats a little faster than usual, you feel a tingle inside, albeit a gentle and totally unsexual tingle. Do not worry. These physical reactions are perfectly normal – they are signs that you are getting on well with another person.

From the outside, you will also be displaying your enthusiasm. You will greet each other energetically, sometimes almost with yells of appreciation. You will use each other's names

a lot. You will show off, flicking your hair
back to show your 'good side'; raising your
voice a little louder to make a point. And to
show each other that you care, you will take
all the nonverbal signs of liking and magnify
them – looking at each other more than usual,
smiling more than usual, nodding more than
usual. The more you both do this, the more
you will both feel appreciated and feel good
about each other.

You will also want to be close to your friend
– literally as well as emotionally. So you will
stand close, face directly, reach out and touch
– seemingly to emphasize a point, but actually
to signal how close you are. You will 'match'
in a whole variety of nonverbal ways – picking
up each other's accents, dancing in the same
style, laughing at the same jokes, wearing the
same clothes, not only to strengthen the

feeling between you but also to show other
people your bond – and to warn them off
muscling in on the friendship.

Interestingly, when you are more sure of the
relationship many of these signs die away –
and there is no need to worry if they do. Your
body language becomes far more like that of a
long-established married couple. You greet
each other with pleasure, but calmly. You are
more at ease sitting side by side rather than
opposite, now that you do not need to see
each other's faces in order to tell what each of
you is thinking. You talk less, and less
excitedly, now that you do not need to
exchange words to know how each of you is
feeling. You smile less, laugh less, call each
other by name less – because you are already
close and do not need these signals to bind
you together.

But despite the fact that you may seem more distanced you are, if anything, more close. You walk along together, totally in step. You and your friend will both move to cross the street at the same time, without noticeable signals. You reach for your drink at the same moment, shift position at the same second. When you reach this stage with someone, you do not need to try any more. Your friendship is deep, and potentially long-lasting.

When Friends Visit, How Can the Environment Make or Break the Evening?

To really enjoy themselves, people need to be able to be themselves without tension. But they will find it difficult to do that if the environment gives the opposite message. So while antique furniture and cut-glass will impress, they will also make it more difficult for guests to be informal. Ornaments that say 'look but don't touch', elegant furniture that keeps people on the edge of their seats, pristine carpets in pure white: all these are death to relaxation. Instead, opt for deep comfy sofas in deep, stain-resistant colours.

Other ways of helping people to relax include the use of colour, heating and light. Warm colours in a mildly heated room will encourage people to sit back and move slowly rather than huddle forwards and talk quickly as they will do if they felt chilly. A too-warm room, though, has been shown to make people irritated and argumentative – so unless you want a fierce discussion during the evening, keep an eye on the thermostat!

Be wary too of bright lighting, which encourages brisk body language totally at odds with relaxed friendly chat; and of lighting that is just too dim – within 20 minutes of lowering the lights during one research study, conversation had stopped entirely and the subjects were mostly interested in catnapping!

Once relaxed, people then want to relate as easily as they can to the others in the room. So do all you can to create an environment that will make everyone feel included. If any chairs are 'out on a limb', move them into the main group. Avoid high formal chairs mingled with lower and more informal seating, which will leave the occupants feeling stranded above or below the conversation. Place chairs at angles with each other rather than on opposite sides, which can make people feel antagonistic towards each other – one reason why arguments tend to happen at the meal table more often than when people are using the 'angled' seating usually found in a living room.

Do not think, though, that people who are in close proximity will naturally interact more positively. If the space they actually have to sit in is actually too small, as happens when two people have to squash together on a cramped sofa, then they will go on the defensive. They will cross their arms and hunch their shoulders to protect their own personal space – and this will not make for relaxed conversation. And if the seating is too deep and soft, then people may feel themselves tilting back or sliding towards others, and this lack of control will also make them feel wary.

Finally, do not forget sound. Music that is too loud will keep people from talking and thinking. Music that is too slow may simply send them to sleep. But music that acts as a background to interaction – providing a slow, soft, relaxing setting that does not intrude – will add to all the other nonverbal scene-setting you have done and help to create an enjoyable evening.

How Should I Use Body Language When Friends Come Round for a Meal?

When your evening with friends includes food, then as far as body language is concerned it is all the same if it is pasta and salad or a five-course banquet. You need to move through a series of phases that ideally need to be managed well if you are all going to enjoy yourselves.

In order to enjoy food, people need to relax – otherwise their stomach muscles will close up and the digestive juices will not flow. So the first part of the evening ideally provides

time and space for people to wind down
– often from a busy day – and also get ready
to eat. So you may allow at least half an hour
between people arriving and eating for them
to relax; sit them down comfortably on soft
seating, perhaps with gentle music; you might
offer drinks and snacks designed to stimulate
the digestive juices.

There is another purpose to this pre-meal
chat: Studies have shown that if people feel
insecure with others, then they lose their
appetite. By allowing time before a meal for
the group to chat, you make it less likely that
this will happen. And it is a good idea, if
someone indicates by her (or his) body
language that she is not joining in, to chat for
a few minutes, putting her at ease until she
seems to be more comfortable.

Then, you can move on to the meal. There is a purely biological reason here why you ideally move to a higher table and more upright chairs. Simply, it is easier to enjoy and digest food if the body is more upright and therefore the stomach and gut are not squashed by sitting. You will probably find, too, that seating people in a more upright way, closer together, raises their energy levels; they may start talking more quickly, allowing their voices to rise, smiling more.

As the food settles, slowly the group will become quieter and slower. As with any animal, humans tend to become drowsy after eating, because all our energy is going into the serious business of digestion. At this point you may want to allow people to leave their upright chairs and collapse onto the most relaxing seating you have, to the accompaniment of really slow and soporific music. Conversation may calm down; people want to be quieter. At this point, if your friends followed their animal instincts, they would simply slide into a horizontal position and fall asleep.

In fact, because everyone but you has to go home, it is best to give people an extra burst of energy to allow them to travel safely. The final ritual drink of coffee not only offsets any possible negative effects of drowsiness on the driver, but livens everyone up so that they can cope with the journey home.

How Can I Say No to a Friend without Alienating Him?

Your best friend wants to borrow your car for the weekend. You may think that he (or she) will dislike you if you refuse.

This can happen. But problems usually only occur because you are anxious about these possibilities or because you are irritated at your friend for putting you in this situation. In short, friendships get chipped away at the edges not because the signals read 'I'm saying no' but because they read 'I'm saying no – and that makes me feel bad about you.'

One danger is this: When your friend makes his request, you feel defensive because you feel bad about refusing. This shows as you unconsciously pull back, turn away, stare angrily, block off your body with your arms, shake your head, let your voice rise irritably. The problem is that all these signals seem to say that you are angry; they are the same kind of signs that apes use to reject unwelcome contact from others. No wonder that, however amicable your words, your friend feels completely rejected for 'only asking'.

Another possibility is that your body language signals to your friend that you feel guilty about refusing. You give a repentant smile, grimace apologetically, hunch your shoulders and look away in embarrassment. But then an interesting thing happens: You expect this body language to improve things, to make your friend feel better about your refusal. But in fact the opposite happens; your friend gets irritable. He does this because your body language signals of guilt are similar to body language signals of admitting wrong and inviting punishment. At the very point that you want to make amends, your friend may feel an almost irresistible compulsion to hit back.

The secret of refusing a request without causing trouble is to combine clear 'no' signals with clear approval signals. In other words, you need to signal nonverbally as well as verbally that you will not do what your friend wants, but that you do want to stay friends.

So be definite about your refusal. Assertiveness trainers, who are usually past masters at the art of effective body language, suggest that you stand straight and say a clear and direct 'no', while looking the other person full in the eye and shaking your head to make the point clearly. If your friend argues, simply repeat your refusal with the same body language – but stay calm, do not look defensive, do not look apologetic.

At the same time, signal friendship. Once your refusal has been accepted, then smile, use a warm tone of voice, add a quick touch – a tap on the shoulder or a pat on the arm – to reassure. If you can indicate by your response that you are saying 'no' to the request but are not rejecting the person, then even if there is bad feeling it probably will not last.

Some People Just Seem to Find It Easy to Get Chatting to Others Wherever They Go. How Do They Do That?

People who are able to 'get chatting' to others, perhaps on a train or in a bus queue, have a special secret. They use their body language skills to let the other person feel secure enough to start talking and to keep talking.

So people who nonverbally seem safe have the best chance of making contact. They look safe: little old ladies find it easier to strike up a conversation than do large muscular men. They dress 'safely': standard casual clothes give off more safety signals than do black leather and chains. They act safely: standing quietly at a bus stop in the middle of the day provides more chance of making contact than rolling up to the same bus stop at midnight in an inebriated state.

People who get talking easily use friendly body language. They are not bowed down with unhappy expressions or nervous twitches. They walk in an easy manner. They do not use protective signals, such as arms across the body and hunched shoulders; or 'elsewhere' signals such as absent-minded gazes or thoughtful frowns. They often have a naturally happy expression, suggesting that they will be fun to be with as well as safe.

The way these people make contact is also part of the secret. Their first step is automatically to look around at everyone they meet; they simply cannot help scanning a room as they enter it, glancing across at the other people in their train compartment, making eye contact in a queue. Then they follow a nonverbal 'safety routine' which allows them, or the people they look at, to withdraw if either is unhappy at what is happening. So if others do not hold eye contact because they feel wary, then the successful socializer does not take things further. Only if the eye contact is returned confidently do things proceed to a second step – another glance across to establish interest on both sides.

Next there is a small smile, a signal even in the ape world that one means no harm. Is the smile returned? Again, if not, then nothing more happens. But if so, then perhaps it is time for a word or two – choosing a safe neutral topic such as why the train is delayed. These 'excuse' comments are made in a light, throwaway tone which does not expect a reply. But if one is given, then both partners smile more broadly, move more energetically, actually shift noticeably closer together to show how well they are getting on.

The conversation has begun, the contact has been made. They will probably keep talking all the way from London to Glasgow!

What Are the Problems I Might Encounter If I Try to Turn Work Relationships into Social Relationships?

Most people make friends at work, but it does have its dangers – even if you never actually reveal your innermost secrets. The different kinds of body language that being friends and being workmates involve may mean that at some point you feel uneasy but you don't know why.

The reason is this: The body language of colleagues is designed to work in a professional context. You have to get things done, not gossip or get emotional. So body language develops to keep you at a distance.

You approach mainly within the social zone of 3.6 – 1.2 m (12 – 4 ft), only sometimes within the personal zone of less than 1.2 m (4 ft), rarely within the intimate zone of less than 45 cm (18 in). You will keep barriers between you, either literally with a desk or chair, or with protective movements such as an arm's-length handshake. You will keep emotional barriers up by making sure that you do not show your feelings too much. You will make sure that your expression and voice do not distract others from the job in hand.

But then you go out to the wine bar together or you end up dancing in a group at the Christmas party. For that short time, in a social setting, the rules are different and all your body language shifts. You do not keep your distance, but huddle together on a pub bench. You smile broadly, you nod, you exchange friendly touches – all signs that you like each other. You do not hold back on the emotions, but laugh or cry in a way that in nonverbal terms is actually designed to make you feel closer to each other. It does not seem strange; it is what enjoying yourself with other people is all about.

Until the morning. If you then try to take the body language of the wine bar back into the workplace, you can find yourself feeling bad without knowing why. A colleague – male or female – moves closer than you want, and suddenly you feel uneasy. Two employees suddenly start giggling, heads together, when in a meeting. Your boss, who was so informal last night in the pub, suddenly seems uneasy at being greeted with a smile and a nudge. What is happening?

Not unnaturally, bodies are getting confused. They are halfway between friendship mode and work mode, so that everyone feels uncomfortable; what they want is one thing or another. And in fact, one way or another, your body language will find a balance. One possibility is that everyone will fairly quickly switch back to work mode and the status quo will be restored; you will make sure not to socialize with each other again except on very rare occasions.

Or, some of you at least will find a way to mix work and pleasure. You will meet out of office hours, but you will take care to use one kind of behaviour before five o'clock and another kind afterwards. To get the best of both worlds, you will learn not to distract yourselves from work by using social body language. At the same time, of course, you will learn not to inhibit your social life by using the body language of work!

How Can I Survive at a Party Where Everyone Already Seems to Know Everyone Else?

You arrive at a party only to find you are a stranger. Everyone seems to be locked in conversation with everyone else, and you are the wallflower. What can you do?

Begin by using your body language skills to identify groups that are actually open to new members. If people are standing in a tightly packed group, shoulder to shoulder, with most people adding comments in confident, loud voices and lots of synchronized laughter, then almost certainly they are already good friends. They may react with

surprise and even some negativity if you try
to squeeze in.

If, on the other hand, people are standing
fairly far apart, talking in turn with quieter
voices and not much movement, this is more
likely to be a temporary group; their posture
and their conversation patterns are literally
leaving space for new members to join in.

Even so, these people will already have a sense
of identity as a group. You will raise hackles if
you simply barge in and start talking. There is,
in fact, a clear nonverbal etiquette for joining
such a group; follow it and you will have a
smooth ride.

Use body language to 'knock' before entering.
Stand just outside the group, but very close;
almost certainly someone will glance round,

spot you and, if you smile reassuringly, will shift to let you in.

Ease gently into the gap. Then stand quietly and watch what is going on around you. You will notice that there is a nonverbal pattern to what the group is doing. One way or another they will be 'matching' each other's posture, gestures or voice levels. Perhaps a number of them are holding their glasses in the same way; perhaps when one person takes a drink, the others do too. To succeed in the group you need to match these nonverbal patterns. If everyone nods, nod too; smile along with other people; groan when they groan at a bad joke. Matching in this way will reassure the group that you are not trying to barge in or take over. So match, even if only for a few minutes.

When you are ready to join in the conversation, again watch the nonverbal cues. There may be a sort of 'pass the parcel' game whereby one person takes the lead, then bounces the conversation to another, who passes it back or passes it on. If you want to speak, start catching the eye of the person who seems to be taking the lead. Keep looking at her (or him) with the raised eyebrows and tilted head that nonverbally says 'Can I have a turn please?' When she feels you are sufficiently accepted, she will pass the parcel to you, winding up her comment and making the 'turn-taking' open-palm gesture that shows you now have the floor.

Take your chance and say something. As you do, look round at everyone in a friendly fashion, to make them feel included in what you are saying. But do not hog the attention; 'pass the parcel' back after a few sentences. You will get your chance to speak again.

Who Is Top of the Pecking Order in My Group?

In every group of people there is some sort of pecking order. This is not to do with being in charge; the team coach, the hostess or some other kind of formal leader is not always at the top of the pecking order. But like birds, humans in groups sort themselves out into a hierarchy with some people being seen as more important because they do things that the group value. Perhaps these people are older, perhaps they score goals more often, earn more, are married, have children.

The pecking order can change, according to what a group is doing. So extrovert Sally may be top of the pecking order when you are at the pub; everyone laughs at her jokes and jumps to it when she suggests getting the drinks in. But when it comes to buying a car, all of a sudden introvert Tom comes into his own because Tom is the world's expert on how to avoid buying a rustbucket; in that situation, everyone listens quietly and respectfully, including Sally.

Most people are never aware of the pecking order in their particular group, but body language always reflects that order. Automatically, consistently, unconsciously people will behave slightly differently towards those 'above' them in the pecking order than they do towards those 'on their level' or 'below' it.

So how can you spot the pecking order in a group you are in? Begin by looking at position: Who sits at the focal point of the group? Who takes up the central position? This person does not have to sit in the highest or largest chair, but his (or her) spot will be the one that draws attention when you walk in the room. After a while, every other chair will end up slightly turned towards it.

What about priority? Who goes first, through a door or in the coffee round? Who is asked first what he would like to eat, or where he would like to go?

What about verbal dominance? Who speaks first, longest, and holds the group's attention most? It may be the person with the loudest voice, or it may be a quiet and retiring individual. But when he speaks, there will be absolute silence.

Who is able to persuade? Whose ideas seem to meet with approving nods and smiles rather than consideration or dubious glances? Who is it who gets copied if he wears something new, buys something different, starts going to a new place?

You may need to watch for a while, as pecking order shifts from one person to the other over the course of hours or even just a few minutes. But by analysing just who in your group is number one in any situation, you will gain real insight into how you and your friends get on with each other, and how you all interact together as a group.

What Are Group 'Roles' and How Can I Spot Them?

A social group is a bit like a sports team; different people play in different positions. This all happens largely unconsciously. People take up roles in a group, act out various parts, fulfil distinct functions. For example ...

Most groups have a resident clown. It is usually a man in a mixed sex group; he makes jokes, plays the fool and does not mind being silly in order to have fun. He moves more freely than everyone else, and often gets down on the floor with the dog or the children. And when shoulders are up, voices are raised and everyone's body language shrieks 'stress' or 'fight', the clown is the one who punctures the tension so that everyone falls about laughing.

The 'earth mother' – only occasionally an 'earth father' – is usually the hostess. She is in the kitchen when you arrive and may spend most of the time bringing cups of tea or slices of cake rather than sitting down and talking to you. She will hug a lot, touch a lot, smile a lot – all approving and reassuring signals. She may also often look worried or frowning because she is always rushing round looking after people.

The 'vamp' can be male or female, and hardly ever means any harm. The female version cares about her appearance more than other women in the group do, and may wear makeup when the others do not. Both male and female vamps talk at length to members of the opposite sex, looking deeply into their eyes in the same way real lovers do, murmuring in soft, low voices, reaching out and touching others.

The 'misery' is miserable. His body language runs through a number of negative emotions, usually a mixture of sadness and anger. Perhaps he sits slumped in his chair a lot of the time; perhaps he is always going for long, angry walks; perhaps he often turns up ill or having had an accident. The misery often needs looking after, having a special chair to sit in, eating special food, going to bed early.

The 'talent' often does have a real gift – maybe for playing a musical instrument, for writing or for working with her hands. She often talks little, just sitting and watching other people. But when she demonstrates her talent – starting to play, sing, make something or perform – then she is always the centre of attention.

Can you spot, from these body language descriptions, whether the groups you mix in contain people playing these roles? And if so – who plays what?

What Can Go Wrong for a New Person Joining an Old, Established Group?

You go with a group of friends for a meal. Two of them bring along their friends, people you have not met before. Then a strange thing happens: One of the newcomers fits in and the other doesn't. It does not seem to have anything to do with personality; both people seem very pleasant. But somehow the group welcomes one of them and totally ignores the other.

What is happening here is this: Each of the newcomers is behaving in a slightly different way – and one of them does not quite fit with what is happening. Any existing group of friends has a way of interacting that is theirs alone. It is down not so much to the group's topics of conversation as their patterns of behaviour. They hug every time they meet, or never, ever touch. They sit in one particular corner of the pub, or they stand at the bar. They wear jeans, or they wear business suits.

Newcomers can easily pick up on the verbal side of group behaviour. They can listen to what is said, then match their statements, questions and opinions to the mood of the group. But newcomers may not be aware of the group's nonverbal rules. And, not knowing these rules, they can make mistakes.

If newcomers carry on as they normally do, then the chances are good that they will not follow the group's way of doing things. They may sit down without checking out the

normal seating arrangement. They may smoke during the meal rather than after. There is nothing wrong in doing these things; it just is not what the group does.

But such actions can arouse the strongest and most unexpected negative feelings. The nonverbal message is that such people are different; the unspoken fear is they might try to influence the group to do things their way. There will be a sense of insecurity and defensiveness, without anyone even knowing why; ranks will close, and the newcomers will be excluded.

If you are part of an existing group and a newcomer joins, you can make it easier for him (or her). First, become aware of what your nonverbal rules are: about clothes, about greeting, about sitting, about eating and drinking, about talking, about 'pairing off', about saying goodbye – in fact, about every aspect of your group's behaviour. Then, give the newcomer a fighting chance by mentioning things in advance, or pointing out, supportively rather than challengingly, if he gets it wrong. People want to fit in; they will almost always change to suit.

If you are a newcomer, the secret is to watch from the sidelines for quite a while. If you take the time to identify, learn and copy the group rules, then eventually you will be accepted. So look and listen for the nonverbal patterns. What do you wear? Is it OK for the men to talk to the women? When is going home time? Then, do what everyone else does, just until they feel safe with you. Sooner or later you will be talked to, listened to, taken seriously, allowed to do things your way – because you are now one of the crowd.

How Does Body Language Help
a Sports Team to Be a Real 'Team'?

The initial step in any team's success is this:
Members need to start thinking of themselves
as a unit, a whole, a group that acts as one.
Clever team leaders know that body language
is often the key.

For example, there is clothing that makes all
the members look roughly the same, and also
makes them look different from the other
teams. There may even be a certain hair style
– very short for the Boy Scouts, pony tails for
the cheerleaders. This common 'look' not only
helps members to identify with their own

group and feel special but also to develop a
sense of competition with other groups.

Next, the team may do lots of physical
activities together – the workout, the training
session, the drill or the rehearsal. This not only
gets them feeling physically good, full of
adrenalin, on a high when they are with each
other; it also gets them deliberately 'matching'
each other – and when humans start moving in
synchrony, they naturally start acting as a unit.

As team members start to feel closer to each
other, they may also start to reveal this by
unconscious or informal matching. Without
realizing it, team members may start to take
on the same ways of moving, picking up each
other's accents, developing 'in phrases', using
special handshakes when they meet.

As the time comes to face opponents, the clever team leader will next start to channel the natural physical energy that the team members feel into the game or competition. Perhaps they will start singing aggressive chants, clapping or stamping their feet – yet more rhythmic matching movement that brings the group together and gets their adrenalin going, ready for the challenge.

Then, by setting up nonverbal, pre-game 'rituals' that involve a certain series of actions performed in a certain way, team members also start to concentrate their minds by focusing their body movements. By the time they are due to 'perform', this skilful use of nonverbal elements should mean that each team member is physically and mentally in tune with all the others, physically and mentally focused on success.

And when that success comes, the most basic reward also involves body language. The first thing that usually happens, when a goal is scored or a point gained, is that all the other team members come up and touch the scorer – the most basic way humans have not only of making another person feel good but also of creating a feeling of closeness to each other.

As they return to the locker room, everyone's happy and relaxed body language shows that they are at ease with each other. What started as a number of individuals has, by skilful use of body language, turned into a cohesive and united team.

How Can I Make a Party Go With a Swing?

If your aim is movement rather than talk, dancing rather than chat, mixing and mingling rather than sitting and interacting, then you need to create a very particular nonverbal atmosphere for your next party.

The traditional guidelines for organizing a party actually get it right: You clear the decks and put away anything valuable, not only to protect your property but also so that people feel able to move more freely, to use open, friendly gestures, to take up lots of space when they move. You provide hard chairs so that people do not sit down for long and have to keep moving and mixing with each other. You turn the lighting down – when you do this, people stop talking. And you turn the music up so that even if guests do talk, they simply are not able to hear each other.

You invite far more people to the party than you believe the space can hold – not only because, as everyone knows, only half the people you invite will turn up! You do it because, up to a certain point, the more friends there are in a room the better those friends are likely to feel about what is happening. For being together with lots of 'safe others' is very stimulating to human beings: adrenalin surges, heart rates rise, sociable touch stimulates and everyone feels positive.

It is important if you are running the party, though, also to keep an eye out for the nonverbal signals that show people are not enjoying themselves. Watch for people standing tensely with their backs to the wall; people who are trying to shut out the sound with slightly hunched shoulders; people who are trying to shut out what they see with downward glances and vague stares; people standing side by side, not talking but gazing out vaguely into the room. Swoop down, carry these people off and introduce them to a small group that is interacting fairly quietly, where they can unwind and find a number of different people to talk to.

As the evening continues you will want to raise the energy level. Make sure the music becomes faster and louder, which will have this effect. Get lots of guests dancing together, because if people move in synchrony they feel good about each other. Do not add too much alcohol, because although at first it may seem to energize people, in the end it may make them either aggressive or sleepy.

As the party begins to end, lower the energy level. Otherwise, after all the excitement and exercise people can feel just too stimulated to sleep. The tradition of ending an evening with soft, low music not only provides an opportunity to snuggle and cuddle, it also allows people to wind down gradually, to start to calm down and get ready to drift off home.

How Can I Get On Socially When I Meet My Partner's Friends?

Is there any occasion more nerve-wracking than being introduced to 'the crowd'? Will they disapprove? Will they be jealous? Will they hate you so much that your partner leaves you?

These are not silly fears. Old established groups can feel threatened by new members, as explained on page 100. And the threat seems greater to them if the newcomer has the weapons of sex and love with which she (or he) may actually lure away an existing member. The group will not feel able to say

anything to you, but they may well reveal
their defensiveness nonverbally by greeting
you with a flat, false smile and handshake
while they greet your partner with enthusiastic
hugs; by leaving you isolated at one end of the
dinner table while they cluster up the other
end; by laughing, joking and touching each
other even more enthusiastically than usual,
just to make the point that their group is
special and you are not part of it.

Quite naturally, your body language will also
go on the defence. In return you will hang on
to your partner literally and metaphorically,
holding his (or her) hand or arm, demanding
the deep eye contact of established lovers,
talking in soft, low loving tones – all aimed to
show that you are a couple and that no one
else can intrude. Alternatively, if you are
feeling annoyed, your mouth may become

tight or sulky, your voice loud or aggressive; then at some point you may well find that everyone else falls silent, leaving your strident tones rising into a secretly triumphant room.

You can largely avoid this scenario from hell if you are aware of the nonverbal undercurrents. Remember that first impressions matter. Underdress rather than overdress because then you may not impress but you certainly will not threaten anyone. If you can find out what the 'group style' is, dress to that, whether it be jeans, dinner jackets, or first one then the other. Gauge makeup or aftershave carefully; if you are the only one wearing them at breakfast, you may be history by the end of the day!

Do not cling to your partner; it hints that your long-term agenda is to take her over completely. Instead, however hard it is, mix. Which of the friends shows, by eye contact and smiles, that she is prepared to be welcoming? Chat to her first; once you have got her on your side, work your way steadily round the circle, spending time with everyone. Leave until last any who seem a little antagonistic, shown by the fact that they do not seem able to look at you, or that they talk to you in flat, expressionless voices.

Once you have made contact with everyone, then act just as you would if you were trying to join any group. Be friendly and approachable. Notice what the nonverbal group norms are and follow them (*see page 101*). Use helpful body language: nothing is more guaranteed to endear you than getting the drinks in, clearing the dishes or doing the washing up.

Finally, steer very clear of anyone who seems attracted to you. If someone sits close, looks into your eyes or 'accidentally' touches your hand, then turn your attention elsewhere. These are all signals that they are sexually attracted to you. Jealousy from your partner or someone else's is the last thing you need in this situation!

How Can Body Language Help Me Realize When a Friendship Is at an End?

Friendships do end, either because of bad feeling or just because you have grown apart. Yet people rarely 'end' a friendship with the same dramatically displayed emotions with which they often end a partnership. So how can you tell what is happening?

Look first at the more obvious nonverbal signals: You are phoning each other less often, spending less time with each other. Your friend is busy more often. Months rather than weeks go by without contact. These things can happen simply because you are both busy, so look next at what happens when you are together.

Where do you meet? If it used to be at each other's homes and it is now a restaurant, then this may be a sign that one of you feels less willing to allow the other into his (or her) personal space. You may feel uneasy about the relationship and this reveals itself in unease about having your space invaded. If the two of you used to meet in a restaurant and now it is always with a group at a film, then maybe this is a nonverbal statement that you do not actually want to interact one-to-one anymore.

If you do meet as a pair, do you have as much attention for each other as you used to? Do you find it difficult to maintain eye contact? Do you find your friend's expression 'glazing over' as you talk? Are there lots of 'escape'

movements, tapping of fingers or flicking of
feet, going on? Are the pauses longer than the
talking – or is one of you doing all the talking
now while the other one does all the listening?
All these signals suggest that at least one of
you does not feel the same emotional bond as
before.

What if the feelings are actually negative?
Have you ever looked up from your meal to
find a fleeting expression of something nasty
cross someone else's face? These 'leakages', as
psychologists call them, happen when a
person's real feelings of anger, mockery or
even fear unconsciously escape and show for
just a fraction of a second.

If you see this, then you may well want to end
the friendship. The most usual approach is the
initial one mentioned above, of simply seeing

less and less of someone. Or, if you do not
mind some bad feeling, you can deliberately
use body language to bring things to an end.
Increase all your negative signals, lose
attention, lose eye contact, fidget and seem
bored. Your friend will get the message,
consciously or unconsciously – and you will
both then 'forget' to make another
arrangement to meet again.

What Is a Goodbye Ritual and Why Does It Matter?

Unlike animals, human beings do not just walk away when they lose interest. They want to meet again, so they want to part on good terms; breaking contact is so significant that, every time, there is a little ritual to accompany it. So when you say end a conversation and say your goodbyes to someone, you go through a whole series of body language movements to bring things to an end.

The first stage is to signal to the other person that you want her (or him) to finish what she is saying – so that you can go. You might find

yourself nodding more often and more quickly, a sign of agreement that carries the hidden message that since she has convinced you, she can be silent now. Maybe you find yourself catching the other person's eye, or half opening your mouth to speak, in the conversational signal that means – 'I want to take a turn; please stop.'

When she has stopped, and you have her attention, you use your turn not to speak but to signal that you want to go. You turn slightly away, look towards the direction you will be going, maybe indicate that direction by a totally unconscious wave of your hand, look down towards your watch as if you are signalling that you have run out of time.

Your companion will almost certainly respond. She will 'match' what you are

doing, copying your look away, turning
towards the exit too, signalling that she
has got the message by nodding, agreeing
with the completely unspoken statement
you have made that you really have to
part now!

If she does not give any of these signals, you
will repeat the whole thing again. You will do
it much more obviously – until finally, in
desperation, you may be reduced to words:
'I really must be off ...'

And then the last stages of the ritual, the
actual farewell. There will almost always be
a smile of acknowledgement, a head 'bow' of
respect, and a slight forwards lean before you
edge away. You will often touch the other
person, in varying ways depending on the
situation. Young people, men, acquaintances,

business partners and those who have spent just a short time together will tend to touch less – perhaps just a pat on the arm or a handshake. Children, women, old friends and those who have just spent a long time together will tend to touch more – a full body hug, or a kiss. Culture too matters – British people are notoriously low on parting touches, while the French always shake hands, and Belgian women offer three kisses on each cheek!

Then, you separate. Possibly you walk backwards for just a moment as you part, keeping each other in view as if in order to delay the parting. As the distance increases, you will start to use gestures and expressions better able to be seen from afar. You will smile more noticeably, raise your eyebrows, use some kind of wave – from the hardly

noticeable finger salute through to the
ultimate in enthusiasm – two waving arms
held high above your head.

Goodbye!